MOST WAY HOME

M O S T
W A Y
H O M E

Kevin
Young

WILLIAM MORROW AND COMPANY, INC.

NEW YORK

It is the policy of William Morrow and Company, Inc.,
and its imprints and affiliates,
recognizing the importance of preserving what
has been written, to print the books we publish on acid-free
paper, and we exert our best efforts to that end.

Library of Congress Cataloging-in-Publication Data
Young, Kevin.
Most way home / Kevin Young.
p.   cm.
ISBN 0-688-14032-7
I. Title.
PS3575.0798M67   1995   94-17832
811'.54—dc20   CIP

Printed in the United States of America

First Edition

1 2 3 4 5 6 7 8 9 10

BOOK DESIGN BY BRIAN MULLIGAN

for my family—
blood, adopted, imagined

CONTENTS

REWARD 1

I. HUSBANDRY

.

HOW TO MAKE RAIN 5

THE DRY SPELL 7

VISITING HOME 9

MISS LUCILLE 14

AN ALMANAC, 1939 17

FIVE 18

SOUTHERN UNIVERSITY, 1962 20

ANATOMY 23

WAKE 25

FEVER 27

II. THE SPECTACLE

BEAUTY 31

THE SPECTACLE 33

The Thin Man's Apprentices 33

Contortionist 35

Brotherhood 37

The Wonder Tongue   39

The Escape Artist   41

Pachyderm   44

Atlas   45

TELLER   51

III. GETTING RELIGION

BAPTISM   55

CONSTANCE   57

REVIVAL   58

SAYING GRACE   60

The Living   60

The Cures   63

The Boiling   65

The Slaughter   67

The Kitchen   69

The Works   71

The Quench   74

The Salon   76

The Preserving   78

WHITEWASH   80

IV. BEYOND THE PALE

DEGREES   85

WHATEVER YOU WANT   86

CLYDE PEELING'S REPTILAND
    IN ALLENWOOD, PENNSYLVANIA   88

DRIVING INDEPENDENCE DAY   91

CENTRAL STANDARD TIME   93

EVERYWHERE IS OUT OF TOWN   94

EDDIE PRIEST'S BARBERSHOP & NOTARY   96

QUIVIRA CITY LIMITS   98

LETTERS FROM THE NORTH STAR   100

ACKNOWLEDGMENTS

Many people have helped on *Most Way Home*'s long journey from inspiration to publication, too many to mention by name. Special thanks must be given to Seamus Heaney and Lucie Brock-Broido, teachers who oversaw and encouraged much of this work. Thanks also to the faculty and fellows at the Bucknell Seminar for Younger Poets for a summer that shaped this book, particularly the last section. For the book's earlier incarnation, Thomas Sayers Ellis, Sharan Strange, and the Dark Room collective proved crucial readers, while Richard Eoin Nash and Hannah Feldman offered vital personal support. Heather McGowan kept faith through the many months between prize and publication. Thanks especially to Amy Machet for sound advice, Susan Sink and Ghita Schwartz for last-minute suggestions, and the folks at Morrow for their support. Last but not least, endless thanks to my parents and anyone else who put me up and put up with me the years my book and I sought a home.

Several poems have appeared in the following journals, often in slighty different versions:

Agni: "Clyde Peeling's Reptiland in Allenwood, Pennsylvania"; "Everywhere Is Out of Town."
Callaloo: "Eddie Priest's Barbershop & Notary"; "The Escape Artist"; "How to Make Rain"; "Whatever You Want" (as "Hundred & Six Degrees"); "Letters from the North Star."

Diaspora: "Southern University, 1962"; "Visiting Home."
Graham House Review: "Degrees"; "Whitewash."
The Harvard Advocate: "Eddie Priest's Barbershop & Notary"; "Fever."
Kenyon Review: "Central Standard Time"; "Driving Independence Day."
Poetry: "The Living."
Ploughshares: "The Preserving"; "The Slaughter."
Village Voice Literary Supplement: "Quivira City Limits."

Several poems have subsequently been published in anthologies: "Eddie Priest's Barbershop & Notary" in *In Search of Color Everywhere;* "Clyde Peeling's Reptiland in Allenwood, Pennsylvania" and "Everywhere Is Out of Town" in *On the Verge;* "Reward" and "Southern University, 1962" in *Testimony;* "Driving Independence Day" in *Letters to America.*

"Reward" and "Atlas" appeared as a broadside and in a fine press edition, hand-printed by the author at the Bow & Arrow Press, Cambridge, Massachusetts.

The great ruptures, the great oppositions, are always negotiable, but not the little crack, the imperceptible ruptures which come from the south. We say "south" without attaching any importance to this. . . . But everyone has his south—it doesn't matter where it is—that is, his line of slope or flight.

—GILLES DELEUZE
Dialogues

MOST WAY HOME

REWARD

RUN AWAY from this sub-
scriber for the second time
are TWO NEGROES, viz. SMART,
an outlandish dark fellow

with his country marks
on his temples and bearing
the remarkable brand of my
name on his left breast, last

seen wearing an old ragged
negro cloth shirt and breeches
made of fearnought; also DIDO,
a likely young wench of a yellow

cast, born in cherrytime in this
parish, wearing a mixed coloured
coat with a bundle of clothes,
mostly blue, under her one good

arm. Both speak tolerable plain
English and may insist on being
called Cuffee and Khasa respect-
ively. Whoever shall deliver

the said goods to the gaoler
in Baton Rouge, or to the Sugar
House in the parish, shall receive
all reasonable charges plus

{ 1 }

a genteel reward besides what
the law allows. In the mean
time all persons are strictly
forbid harbouring them, on pain

of being prosecuted to the utmost
rigour of the law. Ten guineas
will be paid to any one who can
give intelligence of their being

harboured, employed, or enter-
tained by a white person upon
his sentence; five on conviction
of a black. All Masters of vessels

are warned against carrying them
out of state, as they may claim
to be free. If any of the above
Negroes return of their own

accord, they may still be for-
given by

ELIZABETH YOUNG.

I

HUSBANDRY

HOW TO MAKE RAIN

Start with the sun
piled weeks deep on your back   after
you haven't heard rain for an entire
growing season   and making sure to face
due north   spit twice into the red clay
stomp your silent feet   *waiting rain*
rain to bring the washing in   rain
of reaping   rusty tubs of rain   wish
aloud   to be caught in the throat
of the dry well   head kissing your back
a bent spoon for groundwater   to be
sipped from   *slow courting rain   rain*
that falls forever   rain which keeps
folks inside and makes late afternoon
babies   begin to bury childhood clothes
wrap them around stones   and skulls of
doves   then mark each place well enough
to stand the coming storm   *rain of our*
fathers   shoeless rain   the devil is
beating his wife rain   rain learned
early   in the bones   plant these scare
crow people face down   wing wing
and bony anchor   then wait until they
grow roots and skeletons   *sudden soaking*
rain that draws out the nightcrawler
rain of forgetting   rain that asks for
more rain   rain that can't help but

answer   what you are looking for
must fall   what you are looking for is
deep among clouds   what you want to see
is a girl selling kisses beneath cotton
wood   is a boy drowning inside the earth

THE DRY SPELL

Waking early
with the warming house
my grandmother knew what to do
taking care not to wake
Da Da   she cooked up a storm
in darkness   adding silent spices
and hot sauce

to stay cool. She ate later, alone
after the children had been gathered
and made to eat
her red eggs. Da Da rose
late, long after
the roosters had crowed
his name, clearing
an ashy throat
pulling on long
wooly underwear
to make him sweat

even more. *The fields have gone*
long enough without water
he liked to say, *so can I*
and when he returned
pounds heavier
from those thirsty fields
he was even cooler
losing each soaked
woolen skin
to the floor, dropping
naked rain in his
wife's earthen arms.

VISITING HOME
for Keith

Sunnyman:
look there   past
those bitter figs
in the pasture   you can
barely make it out now
but all that you see
all that green   once
was ours

Mama Lucille:
it must have been the summer
before DaDa seemed taller
than everyone   the year your Uncle
Sunnyman was born   the season Keith
stole all your father's well-worn
hard-won   wooden marbles
from a drawer   and shot
them from a slingshot
at the cows   what slow
moving barns
they were

Keith:
DaDa left out in the heat
his share of mornings   only
to return from the market
in Plaisance with nothing   a hog maybe
sometimes a good sow

{ 9 }

but we never had enough
to raise it on   so he slaughtered
what we couldn't keep
gave up the best meat

though he might save
some pigsfeet
for us

   Mama Lucille:
when whitemen came with fear
in the night
they told Da Da he had
   to leave
   that was right
   before the war
and land was so tight
people just got crazy

the mosquitoes that June flew big
as horses

we burnt green wood
and the smoke kept them away

   Keith:
the old house stood
about three four mile across the way
you know
where the road runs now

it was one of those
old shotgun homes
you could have blasted
right straight through it
in one door and out another

but no one never did

Sunnyman:
no one really told me
when it was   they tore
the empty thing down
    Mama had waited a long time
    in that house
    been so many things
mother wife sister queen
guess it wasn't long after Da Da passed on
from that oversized heart
of his   that she weaned me
in this new place   boy, consider yourself
warned: his condition
runs in our family
like you wouldn't believe

Mama Lucille:
it was sunny and my skin ripened
to oranges   I didn't
even have a proper dress
for the funeral
me being pregnant

{ 11 }

with Robert and all
so I wore the one with daisies
figured Da Da would like that
just as much   wasn't nearly
as hot that way
but was it ever sunny

Keith:
there never was a will

Da Da didn't believe in one
he just said the earth
was for whoever needed it most
said we never could own
the land   we just ate
out an ever-emptying hand

some pale man
at the funeral
said the X
by the deed was his
and not Da Da's   and he
could prove it
said we'd have to move
or fight him
and the entire state
of Louisiana

of course we let it go

Sunnyman:
folks say this land will never be Young again
that we have lived too long without
so many things that having
seems too hard   but there's one thing
we can never forget: how the land we were
promised is gone   how home for us
is wherever we're not

MISS LUCILLE

1. All Saint's

she had long since
stopped living
on birdtime

ignoring the coming
the going   those
few who stayed

behind   she kept
to her own earth   bent
far too low sometimes

to notice night stumbling
upon her tiny unfenced garden
when she could no longer see

what was growing in her
hands   she just felt her way
among the steady weeds

pulling what felt too long
to be greens   too short
to be despair

she preserved it all
in jars of vinegar
or placed it deep

in the icebox   who could afford
what bloomed out of season
her fists only knew how quickly

the children grew   tired
of the rhubarb that winter
often brings

so she picked and pickled
and put away   whatever it was
she thought to save   working on

by sickled moons   she swore
there was a man up there
somewhere   and that's why

they kept disappearing

2. Labor Day

She had dropped enough
spoons in her time to know

she was in a family
way. Who needed a doctor

when the metal said it all?
She cursed its silver belly

curled up on the floor, her man
just three days dead & already

giving her another mouth
to fill. No hands to help. Why

leave her another life
to look after when he couldn't

mind his own? But the spoon
just sat there, too dull to see

herself in, too shiny
empty to ignore.

AN ALMANAC, 1939

The midwives all were scarecrows
or spinsters, as if years
of marriage to pain
had left them

without wanting. The other
women slowly turned to trees
thickening their hollows
with plum children

whose shade spilled across their feet.
Had the fathers read
the shifting winds
they too might have grown

to regret this sunless
reaping. But the birds
kept on bringing babies
with such bruiseless skin

that no one saw how far
the children had to fall.

FIVE

No one whispers how old
I might be only you're
still young too young

to be out there in the fields
worrying I am kept inside
hidden among old folks

and freshly cleaned jars waiting
to be filled with figs and spiced
green tomatoes I want so much

to go out there to learn how
the sun can drown the skin
in sweat how the back turns

to shadow I want to go to school
the way the cloroxed and pressed
masters do carrying tin lunch

pails and nickels bright for milk
I have had enough of the burnt
iron skillet of reading nights

from uncle's black-covered
bible secrets I want to know
my number to strut the stony road

shouting I am yours I am old
enough to pick that white
girl cotton to hear that yellow

bell of waterbreak to strap
a thick indigo shirt to my back
each morning at last worn soft

and thin, a childhood

SOUTHERN UNIVERSITY, 1962

for my father

Let's see   first afros I saw   were on these girls from
        SNCC   they had dark
berets with FREEDOM NOW on them   that barely
        covered their helmets
of hair   they sang of the struggle   of the non violent
        demonstration   in town
that weekend   By Saturday it was raining like hell   me
        and Greene
we were home boys   from Opelousas High   we were
        trying to pour in
the last of the blue and white buses this black man in
        town   had let SNCC use
I had my arm in the door   trying to get on out of the
        rain   and so split my
fiveninetyfive raincoat   right down the side   I tossed it
        on the ground
and me and Greene got on just before the bus pulled
        away   When we got
outside campus   ten big beefy white guys   with red
        faces and silent yellow
slickers to their knees   blocked the bus and began
        pounding and pounding
on the door with billy clubs   they tore the door off
        and stormed on
dragging the driver off the bus   throwing him in the
        trunk   they said there
wasn't gonna be no demonstration today   not here   but
        once their lights

disappeared   under all that water   someone said let's
                        go   so me and Greene
and everyone else got off the anchored bus   and
                        walked the four
miles to town   by our soaking selves   When we got to
                        McKays   the WHITES
ONLY five&dime   it was empty as a drum   they knew
                        we were coming
had locked up and gone home   the street was a
                        sea   of umbrellas
and soon as the wind came   which of course it
                        did   my threeninetyfive
umbrella blew in on itself   so I left it on the walk   a
                        broken black
bird   as we started to march towards the city
                        council   Greene's fiveninety
five cardboard shoes   began falling apart   we had
                        started to cross Main
Street   I could just see the top of the white marble
                        building   when about
six cop cars   came wailing out of nowhere   a dozen or
                        so plainclothesmen
jumped out   holding these cans of tear gas   they
                        said   don't even try
crossing this street   go home and stop making
                        trouble   just then the light

changed   turning from red to green   we crossed   the
                    men clubbed us
threw their tears at us   they took out our wallets   took
                    everything we had
and left it on the sidewalk   with our streaming
                    eyes   with the rain

ANATOMY

1 .

deep
in the heart
of the house
the women cook
sweet breads and
simmer

2 .

outside
cold dogs are beaten
by my uncles from
the drowsy porch   back
into the arms
of the strong rain
which drove
them there   will
drive them back
again   to the men who claim
this slanted porch
who drink watered wine

3 .

the lawn
is covered with cars which
slowly burn   tall grasses rise
smoke from each rusty
engine's fire

my great
grandfather looks out
at barren pecan
trees   he nods
  I call those male
  he coughs
  cause they can't grow
  nothing
  at all

WAKE

Jesus tucked with cousins into mirrors
this bedroom reflects more saviour
than self, sees relatives whose names
fade with sun until what's left we call
resemblance, kin   *Sign me up*

for the Christian Jubilee

Da Da quilted in a few feet
beneath crosses & ads for sheriff
the hanging judges he nailed
up himself I lie pillows away
restless, sharing beds like years

of Luckies passed between brown
fingers   Soon he is more cough
than words & sleep is the prayer
carrying him through the night   *Write*
my name on the roll

Not so far ago whites wouldn't
touch blackfolks even dead
specially dead
Mr Bones was the richest
most-sought-after negro in town

I spend the whole of night
counting families, lambs, guessing
at unknown masters who left
this legacy of skin angled red
O I've been changed

since the Lord has lifted me

Dawn, I start sudden as falling
awake during Sunday sermon, half-
expecting to hear Reverend
talking bad bout us Saturday
night sinners, half-looking round

for an amen corner glare

but finding only Da Da's lips closed
brown & quiet as hymnals in the pew
before me, his breath the paper comfort
of church fans: funeral home on one side
smiling family, a father the other

FEVER

I cannot remember the rain
my mother's hands white rum

against my forehead saying
her cypress prayers as I dreamt

of the time Omar and I about set
fire to Mama Lucille's bent paper

house his hands striking
a match then lighting the box

it came from dropping bright
danger to the ground   All we could

do is watch fire spread till my uncle tall
as illness flew to put it out   After

we made him promise not to tell
a soul not ever   Even now

delirious I am a secret my
throat a shivering tree

Once thaw comes a fever
breaks across the rivers

ice turning to heat heat turning
to water   I become an omen   Once

I can stand they burn my sick
sheets my thin tombstone of nail

till the yard smells of ghosts

II

THE

SPECTACLE

It was a most terrible spectacle. I wish I
could commit to paper the feelings with
which I beheld it.

—FREDERICK DOUGLASS
Narrative

BEAUTY

before the Sixth Annual
Coushatta Parish
World Fair
& Spectacle

you run
the hotcomb right
through tight,
crowish hair

a smell of lilacs burning
of ripe, half-bitten plums
of waiting by the fire
for the comb to turn colors

once blue
you take the forked iron out
and pull it through until
your roots come straight

or pull out in plugs baked big
as fists, as hands which made
pies from rotting fruit
and ate them while still warm

your hair keeps on
changing to coal
cooling, quiet beneath
your feet

near pig-tailed sisters
who watch and yearn for
the time
they too will burn

in a light this beautiful

THE SPECTACLE

for Colson Whitehead

THE THIN MAN'S APPRENTICES

Little men born with three heads
of hair, boys of unbroken bones, milk-haters,

boys of lawns & barking roosters, beanpoles
at the sideshow taut holding tents, young men

tying locusts with string, a poor boy's yo-yo.
Father of soft brush, tender-headed boys heading

to barns & avoiding mama's comb, men of prison
haircuts, that bowl around their heads, boys whose ears

outsoar their body, paper airplane kin. Boys of slim
sleep, beds filled with cousins, child of sweet cracklin

& summer spice, boys who ain't hungry, boys living
on love, slipping beneath doors, tightrope

runaways, boys seeing men lynched, boyhood
gone with the circus. Willow men eating soap

to miss the war, seventy-pounds wet, dusky crossing
thresholds, men of harmonica kisses, husbandry,

stomping zydeco night, cigarettes-for-breakfast men,
men of the empty hunt, returning featherless,

hatchet-lunged. Family men, handy men, sturdy
& skinny as rails, hammers waking, John Henry men

racing engines, making do, like love. Men the shade
of bitten apple, red, brown, withering, such wondrous

kite men losing wind, all skin, still soaring, a cross
stretched clear cross the weight of this world.

CONTORTIONIST

see there's this
way of turning
the body back
to bloodless
clay flattening
ear and spine
to paper a dead
language of
trees a way
fingers shape them
selves to copper
rings to promises
with enough
practice any
one can twist
legs into question
marks around
the head in
time sleep
walking on
beds of nails
finding loss
an appetite
for nothing
that certain
secret way
of slowing

the heart for
just one
second but
she can't for the life
of her learn how

BROTHERHOOD

first whitefolks
she'd seen   were Able
and Cane   the Siamese
Twins   the only free
attraction   to be found

at the Spectacle   though
questions did cost   a week
of wiping floors   she made her way
through the crowd of towns
people   the dozens

of kin   who knew what
it meant   to be joined at
the hip   she pulled out
two buffalo nickels   asked
How many hearts you figure

you got?   *Don't know*
said Cane   *Enough*   came
from Able   out of the crowd
a sister smiled   said
to the man

with two faces   I hear
you aint got   but one
heavy heart   & it beats
beats beats   for yall
and yall alone

THE WONDER TONGUE

we took our feet astonished
as Mingha Man, the Wonder
Tongue, pulled the anvil onstage
a hook through his lips

a snared mudfish, he smiled
we cheered him to chomp & lift
barbells, bite the heads off
Depression glass bottles
without breathing or blood

silent, he offered to eat anything
advice, an old wire corset, & a whisper
went round That's Gravy,
Mama Bloodworth's brightest boy
who used to could sing like an angel
dance like a common fool

who went on back east
to school & said his marks
were so good he didn't get a report
least that's what his mama let on
talked his skin so fair

here shirtless blanched
& conked had he truly thought
Hazel's Vanishing Creme
would keep us from seeing

through him? had he pictured
the town passing this
newest attraction by?
maybe he would have been right

but the barker sings so loud
of the teeth & talents
of Miss Bloodworth's lightest boy
we give him a fair
shake & soon, within a word
all of us are sold

THE ESCAPE ARTIST

beyond the people
swallowing fire   past the other acts
we had seen before   we found the escape
artist   bound to a chair   hands tied
behind his back   we climbed onstage
to test the chains   around his ankles
and tongue   watched on
as they tucked him   in a burlap sack
and lowered it   into a tank of water
he could get out of   in his sleep

imagine the air   the thin
man   his skin a drum   drawn
across bones   picture disappearing
acts   the vanishing middles
of folks from each town
the man who unsaws them
back together again   dream
each escape   is this easy   that all
you need   is a world full of walls
beardless ladies   and peeling white
fences   that trap the yard   that neighbors
sink their share of ships over   sketch
each side gate   the dirt roads leading
out of town   the dust that holds
no magic   here your feet are locked
to the land   to its unpicked
fields   full of empty
bags of cotton   that no one
ever seems   to work
his way out of

after the hands
on the clock   met seven
times   in prayer   they drew
the artist up   unfolded his cold
body from the sack   and planted
it quietly   on the way out
of town   at home we still hear
his ghost nights   guess he got free
from under the red earth   but what
no one ever asked   is why
would anyone want to

PACHYDERM

just within the circus
of the tattooed man's
skin stood a still bull

elephant brought
and tamed from
the plains of greyest

Africa nails painted red
acrobats with flesh
colored costumes lying

beneath his harmless dark
foot he worked for applause
and peanuts until he grew

used to the weight of clowns
washed white until their feet
seemed tongues

or pendulums on his back
until he grew silent and
toothless a parlor piano

ATLAS

unveiled he stood
before us a living
map to every
thing he thought
he'd seen each side
show or thirsty
mirage tattooed
to his canvas skin
he stole into the colored
half of each town
the Spectacle went
downing white
lightning & nigger
jazz or even stone cold
sober he'd dance
across invisible tracks
to where the gypsies
drew what they
wanted on him covering
the naked stranger
in sphinxes & pearly
devils for his silver

he began to love
the babylon they
were building he
felt at home filling
his arms & stomach
with their story or
holding the negresses
until dawn showing
them the painted heaven
of his arms the pictures
of dead africans winging
their way home or
seizing the wrists
of whores their O *my*
lords among feathers
& dragonflies

still he never went
past the bounds
of good taste no
design ever slipped
past wrist or adam's
apple no quadroon
ever took his arm
in public with a shirt
on he was quite
respectable it was
only pants off that
they couldn't stop
kissing the thin
underworld of his
legs one buried in
thick jaundice
flame the other
draped in burning
snow that bluish
shade of winter
rarely seen
this far south

but as we circled
around that day
the sun beating
down on the seas
of his shoulders
no one offered
him a mirror no
body showed him
the pale horizon
of his spine or
the boundless
blue of his back
none of us pointed
out the ships full
of people their future
stowed with small seeds
of okra among thick
rooted hair

with his back
to us we wanted
more than any
thing to reach
into the very small
of his spine stirring
the shallows reaching
down among stones
& voiceless shells
diving past that white
hot core to the other
side to where folks
walked on their hands
hoping to find that
continent drowned
beneath calm sight
less skin

later in our kitchen
we told grandma
about the man who
was drawn she stopped
shelling peas & called
us to her undoing
the unmatched buttons
of her shirt she said
when I was carrying
my first & tried
to run the horse
men caught me dug
me a hole for my
child & laid me
belly down in it then
gathered round
like the Spectacle
they whipped me
inside out slowly she
took off her blouse
baring her back
that long ladder
of scars climbing into
her hair *listen* she
continued *what he*
believes he been holding
all these years that aint
a world at all: it's me

TELLER

for A.L.

She read nothing but hands
the color of tea leaves, the Crow
from her daddy's side giving her wild
strawberry skin and a house

on the edge of browntown. She
spent Saturdays blessing brides,
unwrapping cards from red scarves,
spoke surprises into henna
hands, whispering *the heart is just*

a line crossing the palm and love
love is knowing how to clutch it,

when to let go. Long after you crossed
her unmapped hand with silver, long
after taking the back of a lover's hand
or finding the raven's path home

your wings kept time to the fist that is
the heart: pounding, fleeing, reaching.

III
GETTING
RELIGION

BAPTISM

maybe you came here to kill a little
time   or maybe just to get away
from the heat   get away
from mosquitoes carrying off children
but for whatever reason you raced
half-naked to this place

raced each other   raced your fear
of being last   the strongest of you
slinging sacks of stones   dragging
the clawing black cats   along
the trail   to the waterhole
where soon you will get your religion

where one day you will come up breathless
reaching for air   for the preacher
who held you under forever
jesus   was the water choked
with weeds   the left shoes
of fools   of ministers

but today you wade out along the water's
edge   laughing and lying white
boyish lies   let's teach these cats
how to drown   you grin   shirts noosed around
skinny waists   you take the blacks
from the sack   one after

the other   and feed them
to the pond   until the sixth
one is borne out   sleeping
into your scratched hands
his breath awful light   warm
as snow   until you decide to save

this one   to call him yours
and maybe the game has grown
old already   but you can't
help holding   a little fear
that this unlucky
one   might make it

CONSTANCE

In the far room
they strip your
bed clean   stretch
Connie out   along bare
mattress ticking   this
aunt who baked
fruitcakes   into rain
bows   gave them
away   one color
at a time   her shoes now
stumbling over their own
shadows   now twisted
to the ground   for good
you don't want to hear sisters
hiking the dress over
her head   try not to picture
her cameos   placed
in crooked drawers   don't
offer your hands of vine
as the Ladies of the First
Baptist Missionary
Outreach & Choir wipe
her face   heavens   you don't
want to know   if the raven
in her hair has flown
back   if her eyes are still
the color of railroad pennies

REVIVAL

came early with
June, each tent a hot
angel of healing, the Spirit
catching in women's throats
and anointing the lazy eye
of an uncle. You wanted
nothing more than for that
preacherman from way
out west to lay golden
hands upon you, making
your pain that thing
he spoke of

until you became
a testimony circling
the tent on your own. Lord
how you prayed that week
your knees turning into
the hard-backed pews of early
service, each with a brassy
name in its side; how you
went back each

and every night
filling the aisles with
bodies better left
behind. Back then sin
was a coin rubbed
faceless in the pocket
an offering given
gladly, that clear silver
sound everyone
listened for.

SAYING GRACE

for my mother

THE LIVING

1.

After Independence Day
all our toys began to tear
up, school growing sweet

on our tongues. We had
already cut & hoed
the cotton into rows, weeds

piled useless as Confederate
bills. September meant picking
& half-days at Springfield, us colored

grades let off at noon to pick
the valuable white till
nightfall. My hands, civil

& slow, didn't even deserve
my behind on the picking truck,
but Unc Chock ran the thing

& Mama would've killed him dead
if he'd dreamt of trying
to get salty. The money was bad

like all money then, not near
as green or wide. Three dollars
for a hundred pounds, better part

of a day. I barely kept up, hands swole up
like unpicked fruit. No matter when
she started, Frankie plucked fifteen pounds

more, food for two, a new
Easter dress. Summers I turned
so black & bent, all because I'd rather

pick with friends than sling weeds
alone, than stuff my mattress green.

   2.

Winters, when the white king
had gone, we slept like fish, still
moving. We walked back home
for lunch & retraced after school, changing
into our other pair of drawers
before we chored the stove's ash. No one

got gas till after the War. Each November
brought a boxcar from the Atchison
Topeka & Santa Fe; for a share,
Lopez balanced it home on his flatbed,
a whale from the hunt. Once full
of hobos, that belly we burnt kept us

from freezing all season long. Before
tossing each board in, I would run
my hands across the wood speech
of bums, carvings warning
Unfriendly Conductor, Town of No
Sleep. Leftover wood turned

to toys; three boards & somebody's
old rollerskate became a summer
scooter. Bored, what was that?
We were too busy being poor
in that house air-conditioned all winter,
too busy sharing everything, even

bathwater evenings by the pipe stove.
No plumbing, no rats, only mice thick
enough to believe we had more
than they did.

THE CURES

When the colds came
you ended up just sitting
them out. One cough & back
in that bed you went,
laddering up under sheets
cool as heaven. Better
be still—the whole
world moving
past. Shades drawn

tight as dead folks' lids, blankets
heavy as copper pennies
weighed your eyes down.
Measles, mumps, those were
the worst, listening to the murmur
of voices out in the living
room kitchen.

If the cough kept on
you'd get goose grease spread
thick on your chest, then
a piece of flannel
pressed over, made hot
on the same stove

that separated the salve
from saved fat. Old
blankets went to pieces,
either quilts or cures
& the cures worked, bad

as they may have gone down:
flaxseed tea, gooey, gelatinous;
Vicks & Three Sixes for everything
that ailed us. Clean you out
but good. I couldn't eat
oranges for years
or for anyone, seeing how
they'd have us chase castor
oil with wedges wide & forced
as smiles. Sometimes
they'd even add egg yolk, help
it slip quick as okra.

Spring meant spoonfuls of sulfur
& molasses to rid you of winter's ghosts,
sweeping you out like houses
built on crutches to avoid the coming
floods, shooing away all those stray
dogs, unfed, unasked for, underneath.

THE BOILING

My grandfather wore white
suits, would hitch up his favorite
white pony & head to town,
waving his hat like ivory dice,
a small fortune. Even
white folks called him
Mister. Mama had his dark

knuckles, passed down
from Great Mother's set
of black children—with them
she carried seasons & filled
stomachs, lowering that big black
pot perched high on the shelf:

come autumn she boiled
an army's worth of gumbo,
more bone than chicken
lilting up from the mud-
colored broth; summers
that pot fixed all
the crawdads we caught

along the road's shoulder, claws sunk
into leftovers, into meat cubes
strung to sticks. Once a year
maybe turtle soup. After the holiday
hog went, you had two choices
& that one pot: leave the fat
on the skin to skillet up squat

hourglasses of sweet cracklin,
downing it with ginger sauce;
or slice the fat off & stir
& stir till it passed for soap.
No one ever bathed with that,
mind you, our backsides saw
Lifebuoy like anybody else's.

Hogsoap got saved for washday,
each week the dark pot descending
like some Jesus to the stove, filling up
with lye as we cleaned our Sunday
best, clothes simmering, churned
then beaten good & white.

THE SLAUGHTER

1.

Everything we ate was on foot. We didn't have
the Norge or the Frigidaire, only salt to keep.
Autumn's hog went in brine for days,
swimming. You had to boil forever
just to get the taste out. I loved winter
& its chitlins, but boy I hated cleaning.
If not from the hogs, we got fresh bucketsful
from our slaughterhouse kin. White folks
got first pick, even of guts. They loved

that stuff, but to us it was only a season, just
making do. Home, you cut innards in strips,
put water in one end, held the other tight
then seesawed them back & forth. Afterwards
we dumped the excess in a hole dug out
back. I always make sure folks clean them
a second time. Don't eat chitlins
at just anyone's filthy old house.

2.

Chickens went like dusk. Before
twilight, Mama said go get me a hen
& me in that swept yard, swinging one round
by the neck, the pop, then dropping it.
We wrung, but some folks chopped, the chicken
flapping awhile before it fell, headless, a sight.
Feathers we plucked told us that soon
cold would come indoors like greens after

first frost. Everything then tasted so different
& fresh, a sister's backtalk, but I wouldn't want
back those days for all the known world.
No sir. Some nights dinner would just get up
& run off cause I hadn't wrung it right,
others we'd eat roosters tougher
& older than we were, meat so rough Mama
couldn't cut it with her brown, brown eyes.

THE KITCHEN

Heard tell Mama's
white folks were fair
cause they didn't turn her
to bone—only later
did I understand good

wasn't just Unc Chock's hair
but meant the father
didn't want to make her,
meant they paid her decent
so's Mama didn't need

to smuggle home silver,
knife tucked between cuff
& wrist. Still drove me
crazy the way no one
saw clear to pick her up—

then again she probably
would have refused, saying
she liked the walk, more likely
not wanting their family
to know our business. Even now

the son calls her Aunt
as if she never had a whole
nother house full
of mouths. After she'd dusted
& cooked & the dog'd been fed

she fixed herself a little
something, wrapping us
a plate of what whites
called leftovers, but we
knew as leavings:

fugitives of fat dark
meat the mother didn't like;
brown bags of broken cookies
we weren't allowed
to eat till we cleaned

our plates. No matter
how nice Mama's whites were,
the father made her enter
the back way like a cat
burglar, black dress & all—

she'd stay in the kitchen,
the same place her naps hid
between visits to the salon,
back of her head where the heat
couldn't reach, where we knew

she stowed a second set of eyes.

THE WORKS

Broke as we were, we didn't need
fixing. But that autumn the men
weighed down our porch, sweating
in their suits, hats-in-hand,
we answered. Thought at first
it was the government making sure

we was poor. Except only cheese
they offered were smiles
wide as a dollar. Said we sat
on oil & could become rich
as the soil surrounding our house—
that dirt you could barely bury

anyone in, on account it shifted
like their pale eyes. Before ours
waved a wad of bills fat
as a bacon slab, its scent
wafting through the house.
Mama knew you can't get to heaven
digging through earth

& told those reps from Love
Petroleum Works to leave—
but like bad dreams or good
dogs they came back, wanting
to put up a fence, like a fight,
& dig. There, past

the henhouse—we wouldn't
even notice. Said our best crop
may be beneath noses
they looked down at us from.
Who knew what of earth
we'd inherit? Besides

some in town who'd disagreed
found their houses catch,
turn quick to ash. After that
most took what crossed their palms
& moved on. Some swore
they could stay on & farm
for fuel. Mama agreed & signed

though I couldn't figure
what we needed with oil
when we already had enough
to grease scalps, smooth out
my knobby knees. She said
I'd see come spring

when my socks could stay up
later than I did & none
needed darning. Unlike
the poor folks' dentist
who pulled whenever
you had a pain, The Works drilled

through winter with silver I'd never
seen—nothing like the spoons
& washboards Unc Chock
played evenings. The Devil sure
don't like to be disturbed
Mama said in spring

when the drill didn't deliver
& the men quit digging
for dirt that paid, hand-
kerchiefs covering their faces
like matinee bandits. Only once
the well inking over, then empty
as a grave. The drill

just stood there, still, a rickety
crucifix. We watched
rust grow with weeds & the well
widen, our mouths ovens
open & unlit, waiting to fill
with food. Seems all summer Frankie
& I played Miss Mary Mack

back where the word Petroleum
wore off like the promise
of salvation, that Love
Works would hit home
& thick black rain up.

THE QUENCH

Thirst kept with us all
year. Yellow
hands rolled till soft
enough for lemonade, pulp
mixed with sugar
to stop us from wincing.

Water then was clean
as Fifth Sunday sermon.

We weren't the Nehi family
that Frankie's was, heavy
bottles of Coke & orange
nosing against each other
in her icebox, glass pressed
like noses at toyshop
windows. Such swallowed
luxury, small as it was, never got

opened for guests. Guess
that made me kin, her cola brown

flowing in my blood too. Cherry,
grape, my house swam mostly
in Kool-Aid, red staining
our mouths like play
draculas often enough
I don't much
care for it now.

Nickel a packet, six
for a quarter, each flavor

made two honest quarts. Enough
to fill us children with silence
long after the wake, well
past the summer Frankie fell
down the well & stayed
there, soaking up that clear,
careless sky.

THE SALON

Missus King's was more
kitchen than parlor—
before folks got filthy
rich or fancy, we'd spend

mornings beneath Clare's
Beauty Remedy,
the Salon's slipshod sign
from above promising
our bushes of hair would burn

no more. Sisters lined up, dying
to lie back & find themselves
transformed in time
for the Spectacle or city
or sockhop. Frankie & I

would play away
the hours, dissecting
dolls or sharing her pair
of steel skates while older
girls waited to get beautified,

do's fried dried & laid
to the side. A true
kitchen 'tician, Clare
could turn any grain
of hair into flour—soft,

sifted. But no matter
how cool the process
or permanent, Mama left
out Clare's with ears boiled
tender as Indian corn,

& burning as if being
talked about, her head baked
& greazy as after-
church chicken. Wasn't
till Frankie passed on

that my hair came down
from braids, unraveled
like some thick bolt
of fabric from Unc Chock's
general store. Drug

to Clare's I got
her best treatment
for the funeral—hair
pulled, pressed
flat & black as the dress

Mama cut
but I sewed up myself.

THE PRESERVING

Summer meant peeling: peaches,
pears, July, all carved up. August
was a tomato dropped
in boiling water, my skin coming
right off. And peas, Lord,
after shelling all summer, if I never
saw those green fingers again
it would be too soon. We'd also
make wine, gather up those peach
scraps, put them in jars & let them
turn. Trick was enough air.

Eating something boiled each meal,
my hair in coils by June first, Mama
could barely reel me in from the red
clay long enough to wrap my hair
with string. So tight
I couldn't think. But that was far
easier to take care of, lasted all
summer like ashy knees.
One Thanksgiving, while saying grace
we heard what sounded like a gunshot
ran to the back porch to see
peach glass everywhere. Reckon
someone didn't give the jar enough

room to breathe. Only good thing
bout them saving days was knowing
they'd be over, that by Christmas
afternoons turned to cakes: coconut
yesterday, fruitcake today, fresh
cushaw pie to start tomorrow.
On Jesus' Day we'd go house
to house tasting each family's peach
brandy. You know you could stand
only so much, a taste. Time we weaved
back, it had grown cold as war.
Huddling home, clutching each
other in our handed down hand-
me-downs, we felt we was dying
like a late fire; we prayed
those homemade spirits
would warm most way home.

WHITEWASH

The boys just blew
north one April, bought
cars named for birds
of prey, and never looked
your way south
again. Every other blue moon
brought their exotic postmarks
like gypsy moths, labeled
and pinned against peeling
bedroom walls.

No one has done your spring
cleaning, girl.
No one has left his laundry
moored to your lawn.

Those landlocked ladies
never sailed anything
but virgin linen, never stopped air
mailing those damn butterfly
calendars. First you forgot to change
the months, then left them
unopened, cocooning in damp closets.
January would always read Monarchs
and mothballs. Your winters
went on without the sudden
smell of fireworks, without
women dark and necessary as wood
burning stoves.

Someone keeps wringing
your heart out, man.
Someone starts hanging
you out back to dry.

IV
BEYOND
THE PALE

DEGREES

The weather in my head
is always summer: tan,
electric, mosquitoes buzzing
steady as family. My heart
an ant-filled apricot. Outside,
west of here, killing stays
in season, birds plunging
like stones into the pools
of our upturned faces.

And to think I dreamt
the cold might just miss us
this time, that somehow I could
step outside the steady swirl
of leaves & into a season
that never ceases, hands fanning
faces, waving away each yellow-
jacket year. Instead ash
trees bend toward me almost
praying to be lit, craving to be set
free. *Please.* If you must know

I still plan to go out beyond
the pale, just jump the fence
& wade through fireant
fields, keeping on past
my mind's stuttering storm—
it slows, turns thunder then
effortless, suffocating snow.

WHATEVER YOU WANT

for Arnold Kemp

This could be a good day. It starts
without you, as usual; you haven't seen
dawn in years. By noon it hits half-
boiling & the air breaks down. After lunch
even the fans turn lazy, not moving you
or wind. Is it the Negro in you that gets
in the car & just starts driving, keeps
the windows down, your music
bouncing off station wagons, power
windows? Whatever you want

to call it, it makes you feel you own
everything, even the creeping heat. Spin
the radio looking for summer, for love
songs with someone somewhere worse
off than you. Why doesn't anyone
advertise for rain? Instead the personalities
keep talking to prove they are indoors,
cool. By seven the temperature outsails
the price of gas, the movies are all sold out
& you can't get cool for the heavens.

So peel away, head for the edge
of town where the roads turn thin & alone,
speeding to prove you can summon death
like tortoises cracked open in the road
up ahead, the water stored in their shells
running free. Keep on trying to out-race
heat's red siren until radio sings out

Come home, come on home black boy
to your chimney full of birds, to this house
of flame. Evening, the heat holds you
with its aching, unavoidable fingers;
you sleep naked, dreamless to heat.
Windows thrown open as mouths, fan on,
it still feels like a ghost is baking sweet
potato pies through the night. Your favorite.

CLYDE PEELING'S REPTILAND IN ALLENWOOD, PENNSYLVANIA

You must admit it's natural
that while waiting for the three o'clock
informational reptile handling & petting

show, we all imagined a few choice tragedies,
maybe a snake devouring one of the six
identical blond children in the front row,

or the anaconda choking on all five
badly braided girls. I confess openly
we discussed ways in which the obnoxious

crying child in the third row actually wriggled
free of daddy's constricting arms, his head opened
against the ground like a melon & a ripe one

at that. See, in the end the tragedy is all
in the telling, not at the moment when the gator
slips out of Ched Peeling's trusty, thoroughbred

hands & gobbles down a few select
youngsters—preferably the really loud or
beautiful ones—but later, after the ambulances

have sped away & no one breathes
a word. Even when everything is said
& done, I don't know whether only the loud

& really beautiful things get remembered
or most things just grow loud & beautiful
when gone. I can only tell you

that later I thought for hours about Irvy
the Alligator's smooth underbelly & the way
it drove him nearly extinct, how folks once

looked at him & called him desire, a handbag
in waiting. How you won't drive past any Negrolands
on your way through Pennsylvania, or anywhere

else in this union. How while learning about lizards
that grow their tails back, bloodless, I kept
thinking The Colored Zoo may be exactly what

we need, a pleasant place to find out how They eat
watermelon & mate regularly, a cool comfortable
room where everyone can sit around

& ask *How do I recognize
one or protect myself?* or *Their hair,
how do They get it to clench up*

like that? A guide dressed in unthreatening
greens or a color we don't have to call
brown could reply *Good question,*

then hold one up & demonstrate, show
all the key markings. But you must
believe me when I say there is not really

such a place, when I tell you that I held
my breath with the rest at Reptiland, listening
to Ched recite his snakebite story for the four-

hundredth time, waving around his middle finger
where the rattler sunk fangs. You must forgive
how we leaned closer as he described venom

eating green & cold through his veins, pictured
perfectly its slow nauseous seep, like watching
the eleven o'clock footage of someone beaten

blue by the cops, over & over, knowing you could
do nothing about this, only watch, knowing
it already has all happened without you

& probably will keep on happening, steady
as snake poison traveling toward the heart,
the way these things go on by, slowly,

an ancient turtle we pay
to pet as it walks past,
souvenir, survivor.

DRIVING INDEPENDENCE DAY

War built the roads you cross. Men with bad
hearts or flat feet broke rocks, backs, laying
this pave like stateside wives. Strawberries
grow red as handpainted signs which urge you
toward them, a hunger. You never stop, expecting
baskets spoiled bloody or already eaten. Speed
past the Amish boys who don't drink or die

in battle. Flowered tourists pull over to steal pictures
because they can. In the fields the brownest horses
never look back. Only in towns do you slow, steady
when told. Folks in Boalsburg mow their tombstones,
women water flags in Woodward. Hotels keep out
VACANCY the way the Sunday best of a lost soldier

dangles in mother's closet. At the corner store a dime
won't even buy an operator's voice. Ribbons yellow
as hearts clutch to every porch. You leave town thinking
of wars, revolutionary, civil. Where do all the black folks
get buried in this country? German graves push up
against the road, Hackenberg & Gunderman almost touch

{ 91 }

your mirror. Watch for the warnings: Bridge May
Be Icy, the Confederate flag outside Lewisburg.
Past Valentine's Roofing Repair, cemeteries
grow up around the ripe cows. Don't stop to take
it in, just pass by those buildings with flags hung
like black men, those post offices where
the slowest, the most words are kept.

CENTRAL STANDARD TIME

Down below, everywhere, all
the black skycaps have disappeared
since last time, last time being always,
or at least your childhood of air. Gone
like that. At the curb, a mother

overtips the new white luggage hands
as if to say We know who this is no longer
feeding, to say The face on this bill, turned
just so, figured he freed us too. Will you
always wander like an eye,

a rumor? You always seem to be
on the side without a view, only houses
with pools round & unstirred as the water eyes
of the blind, the pale tongues of abandoned
drive-in screens. Must gaining light mean

setting the clock back? The young, balding,
peroxide saint in 5F, the window,
reads his Bible with easy-reference finger guides
to all the psalms, mouthing words
like some cross-country horror movie

minus airplane crash, that you don't
pay to hear. Only watch, guess what
those tongues must be saying,
what monsters they must be
warning us about.

EVERYWHERE IS OUT OF TOWN

for Maceo Parker & the JB Horns

Beanville. Tea
party. Five black cats
& a white boy. Chitlin
circuit. Gravy colored suits,
preacher stripes. Didn't
know you could buy
muttonchops these days.
Afros. Horns slung
round necks like giant
ladles. Dressing. Uptempo
blessing: *Good God*

everywhere! We bow our
heads before the band
lets loose. Drummer unknown
as a hymn's third verse.
Older woman pushes toward
the front, catching the spirit
like the crazy lady at church
six scotches later. Communion

breath. Hands waving. Sweaty
face rags, post-sermon
mop, suicidal white girls crying
like the newly baptized. All that
water. Play it. Swing
it. *Be suggestive.* Request
"Chicken" & "Pass the Peas"
like we used to say. Have mercy!
Thanksgiving's back in town

& we're all crammed in the club white
as the walls of a church basement. Feet
impatient as forks. Only ten bucks
a plate for this leftover band. Thigh,
drumsticks, neck. Dark meat.

EDDIE PRIEST'S
BARBERSHOP & NOTARY

Closed Mondays

is music   is men
off early from work   is waiting
for the chance at the chair
while the eagle claws holes
in your pockets   keeping
time   by the turning
of rusty fans   steel flowers with
cold breezes   is having nothing
better to do   than guess at the years
of hair   matted beneath the soiled caps
of drunks   the pain of running
a fisted comb through stubborn
knots   is the dark dirty low
down blues   the tender heads
of sons fresh from cornrows   all
wonder at losing   half their height
is a mother gathering hair   for good
luck   for a soft wig   is the round
difficulty of ears   the peach
faced boys asking Eddie
to cut in parts and arrows
wanting to have their names read
for just a few days   and among thin
jazz   is the quick brush of a done
head   the black flood around
your feet   grandfathers
stopping their games of ivory

dominoes   just before they reach the bone
yard   is winking widowers announcing
cut it clean off   I'm through courting
and hair only gets in the way   is the final
spin of the chair   a reflection of
a reflection   that sting of wintergreen
tonic   on the neck of a sleeping snow
haired man   when you realize it is
your turn   you are next

QUIVIRA CITY LIMITS

for Thomas Fox Averill

Pull over. Your car with its slow
breathing. Somewhere outside Topeka

it suddenly all matters again,
those tractors blooming rust

in the fields only need a good coat
of paint. Red. You had to see

for yourself, didn't you; see that the world
never turned small, transportation

just got better; to learn
we can't say a town or a baseball

team without breathing in
a dead Indian. To discover why Coronado

pushed up here, following the guide
who said he knew fields of gold,

north, who led them past these plains,
past buffaloes dark as he was. Look.

Nothing but the wheat, waving them
sick, a sea. While they strangle

him blue as the sky above you
The Moor must also wonder

when will all this ever be enough?
this wide open they call discovery,

disappointment, this place my
thousand bones carry, now call home.

LETTERS FROM
THE NORTH STAR

Dear you: the lights here ask
nothing, the white falling
around my letters silent,
unstoppable. I am writing this
from the empty stomach of sleep

where nothing but the cold
wonders where you're headed;
nobody here peels heads sour
and cheap as lemon, and only
the car sings *AM* the whole

night through. In the city,
I have seen children half-
bitten by wind. Even trains
arrive without a soul
to greet them; things do

not need me here, this world
dances on its own. Only bridges
beg for me to make them
famous, to learn what I had
almost forgotten of flying,

of soaring free, south,
down. So long. Xs, Os.

Kevin Young has published widely, his poems appearing in journals such as *Kenyon Review, Ploughshares, Agni Review,* and *Poetry* and the anthologies *On the Verge, In Search of Color Everywhere, Testimony,* and *Letters to America.* After a migratory childhood, Young attended Harvard University, receiving its Academy of American Poets Prize. He has held a Stegner Fellowship in poetry at Stanford University, as well as residencies at the Bucknell Seminar for Younger Poets and the MacDowell Colony. A member of the Boston-based Dark Room collective, Young is currently completing an M.F.A. at Brown University in Providence, Rhode Island.